EASY POP MELODIES
FOR VIOLA

ISBN 978-1-4803-8436-1

HAL•LEONARD®
CORPORATION

7777 W. BLUEMOUND RD. P.O. BOX 13819 MILWAUKEE, WI 53213

Visit Hal Leonard Online at
www.halleonard.com

ALL MY LOVING

VIOLA

Words and Music by JOHN LENNON
and PAUL McCARTNEY

BEAUTY AND THE BEAST

from Walt Disney's BEAUTY AND THE BEAST

VIOLA

Lyrics by HOWARD ASHMAN
Music by ALAN MENKEN

BLOWIN' IN THE WIND

VIOLA

Words and Music by
BOB DYLAN

CAN YOU FEEL THE LOVE TONIGHT

from Walt Disney Pictures' THE LION KING

VIOLA

Music by ELTON JOHN
Lyrics by TIM RICE

CAN'T HELP FALLING IN LOVE

VIOLA

Words and Music by GEORGE DAVID WEISS,
HUGO PERETTI and LUIGI CREATORE

CLOCKS

Words and Music by GUY BERRYMAN,
JON BUCKLAND, WILL CHAMPION
and CHRIS MARTIN

VIOLIN

DAYDREAM BELIEVER

VIOLA

Words and Music by
JOHN STEWART

Moderately

Oh, I could hide 'neath the wings of the
You once thought of me as a

blue - bird as she sings. The six o - 'clock a - larm would nev - er
white knight on his steed. Now you know how hap - py I can

ring. But it rings and I rise, wipe the
be. Oh, and our good times start and end with - out

sleep out of my eyes. My shav - ing ra - zor's
dol - lar one to spend. But how much, ba - by,

cold _____ and it stings.)
do we real - ly need?)   Cheer up, sleep - y

Jean. Oh, what can it mean to a day - dream be -

liev - er and a home - com - ing queen?

DON'T KNOW WHY

VIOLA

Words and Music by
JESSE HARRIS

DON'T STOP BELIEVIN'

VIOLA

Words and Music by STEVE PERRY,
NEAL SCHON and JONATHAN CAIN

EDELWEISS
from THE SOUND OF MUSIC

VIOLA

Lyrics by OSCAR HAMMERSTEIN II
Music by RICHARD RODGERS

EIGHT DAYS A WEEK

VIOLA

Words and Music by JOHN LENNON
and PAUL McCARTNEY

Moderately fast

1., 3. Ooh, I need your love, babe; guess you know it's true.
2. Love you ev - 'ry day, girl; al - ways on my mind.

Hope you need my love, babe, just like I need you.
One thing I can say, girl: love you all the time.

Hold me, ___ love me, ___ hold me, ___ love me. ___

Ain't got noth - in' but love, babe, eight days a week. ___

Eight days a week I love ___ you.

Eight days a week is not e - nough to show I care. ___

EVERY BREATH YOU TAKE

VIOLA

Music and Lyrics by
STING

FIREFLIES

VIOLA

Words and Music by
ADAM YOUNG

GEORGIA ON MY MIND

VIOLA

Words by STUART GORRELL
Music by HOAGY CARMICHAEL

IN MY LIFE

VIOLA

Words and Music by JOHN LENNON
and PAUL McCARTNEY

HEY, SOUL SISTER

VIOLA

Words and Music by PAT MONAHAN,
ESPEN LIND and AMUND BJORKLAND

HOT N COLD

VIOLA

Words and Music by KATY PERRY,
MAX MARTIN and LUKASZ GOTTWALD

ISN'T SHE LOVELY

VIOLA

Words and Music by
STEVIE WONDER

THE LETTER

VIOLA

Words and Music by
WAYNE CARSON THOMPSON

LIKE A VIRGIN

VIOLA

Words and Music by BILLY STEINBERG
and TOM KELLY

THE LOOK OF LOVE

from *CASINO ROYALE*

VIOLA

Words by HAL DAVID
Music by BURT BACHARACH

LOVE ME TENDER

VIOLA

Words and Music by ELVIS PRESLEY
and VERA MATSON

MR. TAMBOURINE MAN

VIOLA

Words and Music by
BOB DYLAN

LOVE STORY

VIOLA

Words and Music by
TAYLOR SWIFT

MOON RIVER

from the Paramount Picture BREAKFAST AT TIFFANY'S

Words by JOHNNY MERCER
Music by HENRY MANCINI

VIOLA

MORNING HAS BROKEN

Words by ELEANOR FARJEON
Music by CAT STEVENS

VIOLA

MY CHERIE AMOUR

VIOLA

Words and Music by STEVIE WONDER,
SYLVIA MOY and HENRY COSBY

MY GIRL

VIOLA

Words and Music by WILLIAM "SMOKEY" ROBINSON
and RONALD WHITE

MY FAVORITE THINGS

from THE SOUND OF MUSIC

VIOLA

Lyrics by OSCAR HAMMERSTEIN II
Music by RICHARD RODGERS

Brightly

F#m

Rain - drops on ros - es and whis - kers on kit - tens,
Cream - col - ored po - nies and crisp ap - ple stru - dels,

Dmaj7

bright cop - per ket - tles and warm wool - en mit - tens,
door - bells and sleigh - bells and schnit - zel with noo - dles,

Bm7   E9   C#m7(no5)   D/F#

brown pa - per pack - ag - es tied up with strings;
wild geese that fly with the moon on their wings;

A/E   D   Bm7b5   C#7

these are a few of my fa - vor - ite things.

1.
F#m

2.
F#

F#

Girls in white dress - es with blue sat - in sash - es,

MY HEART WILL GO ON

(Love Theme from 'Titanic')

from the Paramount and Twentieth Century Fox Motion Picture TITANIC

VIOLA

Music by JAMES HORNER
Lyric by WILL JENNINGS

NIGHTS IN WHITE SATIN

VIOLA

Words and Music by
JUSTIN HAYWARD

NOWHERE MAN

VIOLA

Words and Music by JOHN LENNON
and PAUL McCARTNEY

PUFF THE MAGIC DRAGON

VIOLA

Words and Music by LENNY LIPTON
and PETER YARROW

RAINDROPS KEEP FALLIN' ON MY HEAD
from BUTCH CASSIDY AND THE SUNDANCE KID

VIOLA

Lyric by HAL DAVID
Music by BURT BACHARACH

Moderate Shuffle

Rain - drops keep fall - in' on my head, and just like the guy whose feet are
did me some talk - in' to the sun, and I said I did - n't like the
Rain - drops keep fall - in' on my head, but that does - n't mean my eyes will

too big for his bed, noth - in' seems to fit. Those
way he got things done, sleep - in' on the job. Those
soon be turn - in' red. Cry - in's not for me 'cause

rain - drops are fall - in' on my head, they keep fall - in'. So I just
rain - drops are fall - in' on my head, they keep fall - in'.
I'm nev - er gon - na stop the rain by com - plain - in'.

But there's one thing I know: __ the blues __ they send __ to meet __

__ me won't de - feat __ me. It won't be long __ till

hap - pi - ness __ steps up __ to greet __ me. __

CODA

Be - cause I'm free, noth - in's wor - ry - in' me. __

SCARBOROUGH FAIR/CANTICLE

VIOLA

Arrangement and Original Counter Melody by PAUL SIMON
and ARTHUR GARFUNKEL

SOMEWHERE OUT THERE

from AN AMERICAN TAIL

VIOLA

Music by BARRY MANN and JAMES HORNER
Lyric by CYNTHIA WEIL

THE SOUND OF MUSIC

from THE SOUND OF MUSIC

VIOLA

Lyrics by OSCAR HAMMERSTEIN II
Music by RICHARD RODGERS

47

STRANGERS IN THE NIGHT
adapted from A MAN COULD GET KILLED

Viola

Words by CHARLES SINGLETON and EDDIE SNYDER
Music by BERT KAEMPFERT

SUNSHINE ON MY SHOULDERS

VIOLA

Words by JOHN DENVER
Music by JOHN DENVER, MIKE TAYLOR
and DICK KNISS

SWEET CAROLINE

VIOLA

Words and Music by
NEIL DIAMOND

Moderately

Where it be - gan,
Was in the spring,

I can't be - gin to know - ing,
and spring be - came the sum - mer.

but then, I know it's grow - ing strong.
Who'd have be - lieved you'd come _ a -

long.

Hands, _____

touch-ing hands, _____

reach-ing out,

touch-ing me,

touch-ing you. _____

Sweet Car - o - line, _____
I've been in - clined _____

good times nev - er seemed so
to be - lieve they nev - er

good.

would. Oh, no, no.

TILL THERE WAS YOU

from Meredith Willson's THE MUSIC MAN

VIOLA

By MEREDITH WILLSON

THE TIMES THEY ARE A-CHANGIN'

VIOLA

Words and Music by
BOB DYLAN

Come gath - er 'round, peo - ple, wher - ev - er you roam,
writ - ers and crit - ics who prophe-size with your pen,

and ad - mit that the wa - ters a - round you have
and keep your eyes wide; the chance won't come a -

grown, and ac - cept it that soon you'll be drenched to the
gain. And don't speak too soon, for the wheel's still in

bone. If your time to you is worth
spin. And there's no tell - in' who that it's

sav - in', then you bet - ter start swim - ming or you'll
nam - in', for the los - er now will be

sink like a stone, for the times, they are a -
lat - er to win,

chang - in'. Come

UNCHAINED MELODY

VIOLA

Lyric by HY ZARET
Music by ALEX NORTH

Oh, my love, my dar - ling, I've hun - gered for your
Time goes by so slow - ly, and time can do so

touch a long, lone - ly time. _____
much. Are

you still mine? _____ I need your love, _____

_____ I need your love. _____ God speed your love

_____ to me. _____ **Fine** Lone - ly riv - ers
Lone - ly riv - ers

flow to the sea, to the sea, to the o - pen
sigh, "Wait for me, wait for me. I'll be com - ing

arms of the sea. _____ **D.C. al Fine**
home; wait for **(take repeat)**
me." _____

TOMORROW

from The Musical Production ANNIE

VIOLA

Lyric by MARTIN CHARNIN
Music by CHARLES STROUSE

The sun - 'll come out to - mor - row. Bet your bot - tom dol - lar that to - mor - row there'll be sun. Just think - ing a - bout to - mor - row clears a - way the cob - webs and the sor - row till there's none. When I'm stuck with a day that's gray and lone - ly, I just stick out my chin and grin and say,

55

VIVA LA VIDA

VIOLA

Words and Music by GUY BERRYMAN,
JON BUCKLAND, WILL CHAMPION
and CHRIS MARTIN

WE ARE THE WORLD

VIOLA

Words and Music by LIONEL RICHIE
and MICHAEL JACKSON

WHAT A WONDERFUL WORLD

VIOLA

Words and Music by GEORGE DAVID WEISS
and BOB THIELE

WONDERWALL

VIOLA

Words and Music by
NOEL GALLAGHER

YOU ARE THE SUNSHINE OF MY LIFE

VIOLA

Words and Music by
STEVIE WONDER

YOU'VE GOT A FRIEND

VIOLA

Words and Music by
CAROLE KING

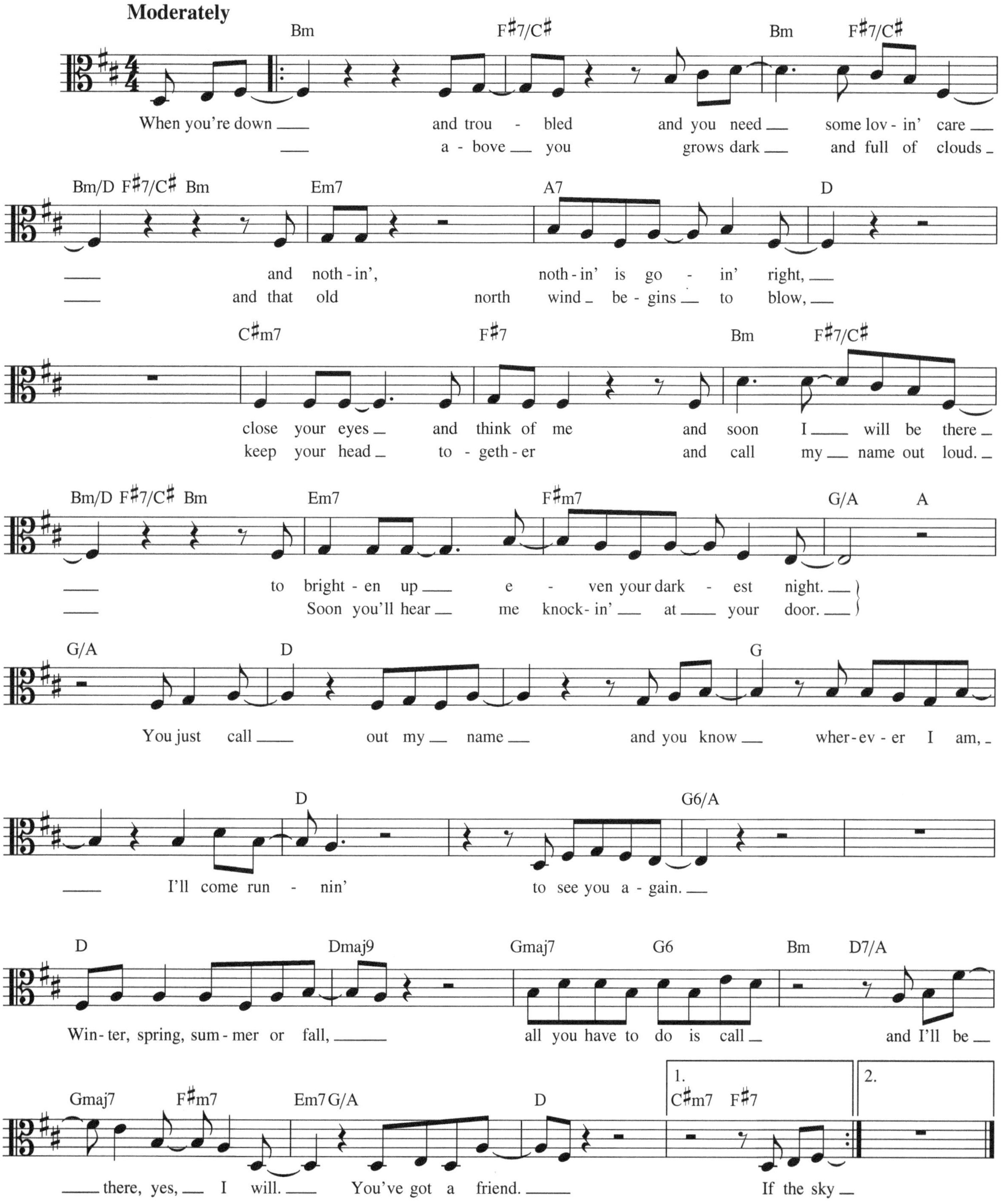

Audio Access Included

HAL•LEONARD
EASY INSTRUMENTAL PLAY-ALONG

- Perfect for beginning players
- Carefully edited to include only the notes and rhythms that students learn in the first months playing their instrument
- Great-sounding demonstration and play-along tracks
- Audio tracks can be accessed online for download or streaming, using the unique code inside the book

DISNEY
Book with Online Audio Tracks

The Ballad of Davy Crockett • Can You Feel the Love Tonight • Candle on the Water • I Just Can't Wait to Be King • The Medallion Calls • Mickey Mouse March • Part of Your World • Whistle While You Work • You Can Fly! You Can Fly! You Can Fly! • You'll Be in My Heart (Pop Version).

00122184	Flute	$9.99
00122185	Clarinet	$9.99
00122186	Alto Sax	$9.99
00122187	Tenor Sax	$9.99
00122188	Trumpet	$9.99
00122189	Horn	$9.99
00122190	Trombone	$9.99
00122191	Violin	$9.99
00122192	Viola	$9.99
00122193	Cello	$9.99
00122194	Keyboard Percussion	$9.99

CLASSIC ROCK
Book with Online Audio Tracks

Another One Bites the Dust • Born to Be Wild • Brown Eyed Girl • Dust in the Wind • Every Breath You Take • Fly like an Eagle • I Heard It Through the Grapevine • I Shot the Sheriff • Oye Como Va • Up Around the Bend.

00122195	Flute	$9.99
00122196	Clarinet	$9.99
00122197	Alto Sax	$9.99
00122198	Tenor Sax	$9.99
00122201	Trumpet	$9.99
00122202	Horn	$9.99
00122203	Trombone	$9.99
00122205	Violin	$9.99
00122206	Viola	$9.99
00122207	Cello	$9.99
00122208	Keyboard Percussion	$9.99

CLASSICAL THEMES
Book with Online Audio Tracks

Can Can • Carnival of Venice • Finlandia • Largo from Symphony No. 9 ("New World") • Morning • Musette in D Major • Ode to Joy • Spring • Symphony No. 1 in C Minor, Fourth Movement Excerpt • Trumpet Voluntary.

00123108	Flute	$9.99
00123109	Clarinet	$9.99
00123110	Alto Sax	$9.99
00123111	Tenor Sax	$9.99
00123112	Trumpet	$9.99
00123113	Horn	$9.99
00123114	Trombone	$9.99
00123115	Violin	$9.99
00123116	Viola	$9.99
00123117	Cello	$9.99
00123118	Keyboard Percussion	$9.99

CHRISTMAS CAROLS
Book with Online Audio Tracks

Angels We Have Heard on High • Christ Was Born on Christmas Day • Come, All Ye Shepherds • Come, Thou Long-Expected Jesus • Good Christian Men, Rejoice • Jingle Bells • Jolly Old St. Nicholas • Lo, How a Rose E'er Blooming • On Christmas Night • Up on the Housetop.

00130363	Flute	$9.99
00130364	Clarinet	$9.99
00130365	Alto Sax	$9.99
00130366	Tenor Sax	$9.99
00130367	Trumpet	$9.99
00130368	Horn	$9.99
00130369	Trombone	$9.99
00130370	Violin	$9.99
00130371	Viola	$9.99
00130372	Cello	$9.99
00130373	Keyboard Percussion	$9.99

POP FAVORITES
Book with Online Audio Tracks

Achy Breaky Heart (Don't Tell My Heart) • I'm a Believer • Imagine • Jailhouse Rock • La Bamba • Louie, Louie • Ob-La-Di, Ob-La-Da • Splish Splash • Stand by Me • Yellow Submarine.

00232231	Flute	$9.99
00232232	Clarinet	$9.99
00232233	Alto Sax	$9.99
00232234	Tenor Sax	$9.99
00232235	Trumpet	$9.99
00232236	Horn	$9.99
00232237	Trombone	$9.99
00232238	Violin	$9.99
00232239	Viola	$9.99
00232240	Cello	$9.99
00233296	Keyboard Percussion	$9.99

HAL•LEONARD®
www.halleonard.com

0917